27 Questions to Ask Yourself _BEFORE_ Starting a Business

Save Yourself Time, Money, and Headaches

Bob Wilson, M.Ed.

Copyright © 2021 Robert R. Wilson
All Rights Reserved

Cover design: Pradeep from CoverCreators

Dedicated to those who dream of having a successful business.

Contents

Preface _____ 6

Introduction _____ 9

Chapter 1: Which of These Three is Your Main Reason for Being in Business? _____ 18

Chapter 2: Who Do I Need to Pay Besides Employees? _____ 21

Chapter 3: Who Else Can Provide Wisdom and Insights? _____ 28

Chapter 4: Make it Legal _____ 31

Chapter 5: Is it Needed? _____ 33

Chapter 6: Ability to Pay _____ 38

Chapter 7: Will They Pay? _____ 40

Chapter 8: Competition _____ 44

Chapter 9: Plan B and Beyond __ 50

Chapter 10: Self-Employment __ 52

Chapter 11: Business Model ____ 54

Chapter 12: Ideal Customer ____ 58

Chapter 13: Good Customer ___ 63

Chapter 14: Nightmare Customer _____ 65

Chapter 15: Get the Best, Forget the Rest _____ 68

Chapter 16: Define Your Absolutes _____ 73

Chapter 17: What's Unique? ___75

Chapter 18: Customer Interactions _____ 79

Chapter 19: Social Media Platform Strategy: Narrow vs. Wide_____84

Chapter 20: Product, Service, or Both? _____ 87

Chapter 21: Offering Guarantees? _____ 90

Chapter 22: Returns and Warranties _____ 93

Chapter 23: Billing and Payments _____ 97

Chapter 24: Define Security Measures   100

Chapter 25: Insurance Needs _112

Chapter 26: Determine the End Game _____ 115

Chapter 27: Initial Metrics _____ 119

Summary _____ 124

Appendix: Recommended Reading _____ 130

About the Author _____ 133

Other Books by Bob _____ 134

Acknowledgments _____ 135

References _____ 137

Preface

In addition to running my own business as a Career and Business Coach, I enjoyed teaching a Small Business Start-Up class. I taught this class for several years through a community college and had the best of both worlds. The school provided the curriculum and allowed me to supplement the course with materials of my choosing.

One of the questions that kept surfacing in class was:

"How can I best prepare for small business ownership?"

In other words, what steps can I take before I open for business to help increase my chances of success?

This prompted me to create a list of questions that one can ask themselves before launching a business. As you can imagine, the list started small at a half-dozen questions. With each passing semester, I added to the list and refined the questions until I reached the 27 questions you see today.

As you read this book, I strongly encourage you to take the time to write (or type) your answers to these 27 questions. One benefit of capturing your answers is it can give you a fresh perspective. You may see your business in a new light that propels you to approach things differently.

Another potential benefit is it can help you formulate additional questions to add to the list. Even if neither of those things happens, recording your answers can provide more clarity and be great input into creating your business plan, regardless of whether it's a formal or an informal one.

Introduction

This book is intended to be used **_before_** you launch your business. I anticipate some of you may have already launched your business and are wondering if this book can help you too.

The answer is yes. Answering these questions after you're up-and-running can be helpful too. If you do so, just be careful that you don't get caught up being self-critical about past decisions. Deal with "the now" and use the questions to help you make your business become better going forward.

But, as I'm sure you can tell from the title, this book will provide the most benefit to those who haven't yet launched.

When it comes to starting a small business, it is both exciting and terrifying. Sifting through all the advice from so-called experts and how that applies to your situation can be mind-boggling.

One thing is certain. There isn't a single recipe that works for everyone. Starting a small business is much like life. There are many variables, there are no guarantees, there will be surprises, and you will have to be flexible and adaptable.

Steve Blank, a serial entrepreneur, author, and founder of the Lean Startup Movement, is credited with saying that business plans don't survive first contact with customers (Blank, 2010).

Based on the business owners I've coached, taught, and talked with, this quote is right on target.

There are no guarantees. So, any program or plan that guarantees success for a small business is one to avoid.

The point of Mr. Blank's statement isn't to skip planning. Instead, the point is when you plan, know that your plan will change, so build flexibility into your planning process.

This may sound discouraging but try not to see it that way. Owning a small business can be a very rewarding experience. Just be prepared to put in the effort. A big key is planning, anticipating, and taking steps to reduce risks.

I have often been known to say a business owner is like a cross between an architect and a mad scientist. You need structure, procedures and must weigh out your risks. At the same time, you must be prepared to experiment and try new things. If your inner mad scientist comes up with a crazy, out-of-the-box idea, don't just dismiss it. Instead, let your inner architect review the idea, finding ways to limit the risk. In this way, you get a nice blend of innovation and practicality.

If you don't like change, you might want to re-think the idea of having your own business.

It may seem like I am trying to scare you off, but that isn't the case. My goal is to help you be as prepared as possible for this journey.

One of the best ways to be prepared is to ask yourself the right questions and answer them as honestly as possible.

A huge part of helping you prepare is giving you the straight scoop. That is, giving you both the good and the bad: what you want to hear and what you don't.

But as I've often experienced, the things we least want to hear are the things that benefit us the most. Take a minute and reflect on that.

What you least want to hear is what can help you the most.

Unfortunately, there seems to this growing belief that if you "find your passion," then everything else will fall into place. Sorry, it doesn't work that way. Find your passion, then work hard to realize it. If it truly is your passion, then working hard at it will be less difficult than with something that isn't your passion. Either way, it's still hard work.

And, frankly, it should be hard work. Think about it. How can anything worthwhile be easy? I can't think of a single worthwhile thing that doesn't involve hard work. I believe you will find that to be true too.

Being realistic about business ownership increases your chances of success dramatically.

This book contains 27 questions for you to answer before you go into business for yourself. Each chapter is devoted to one of the questions.

The questions are arranged in what I consider a logical order. If answering them in a different order would work better for you, then please do so. As with anything within this book, modify it to best suit your specific situation and needs.

When answering these 27 questions, you will gain the most if you are brutally honest with yourself.

In answering these questions, you may discover business ownership isn't for you. If so, I encourage you to avoid seeing this as a failure. Business ownership isn't for everyone. There are plenty of people that realized this only after investing lots of time and money. If you find out it's not for you early in the process, consider yourself fortunate.

On the other hand, if business ownership still looks like a fit for you, then in answering these questions, you'll be better prepared to know what adjustments to make. So, with that, let's dive into the 27 questions.

Chapter 1: Which of These Three is Your Main Reason for Being in Business?

What is my primary reason for starting my business?

There are three primary reasons for being in business:

a. Make lots of money

b. Help others

c. Have power

Your reason can be a combination of these things. But everyone has one reason that outweighs the others, at least by a small amount.

For example, if you want to become famous or "be in charge," – those would fit within the power category.

Be careful here that you don't just rush into answering "help others."

That is a popular choice because cultural and societal norms often portray goals focused on money or power as selfish. There is nothing wrong with money or power goals if one doesn't abuse their money or power.

Let me assure you, any of these answers are valid. I'm not asking you to shout your answer from the rooftops. Rather, just answer honestly to yourself.

An honest answer makes it easier to choose the best strategies, business models, and approaches for your business. Take the time to identify which of the three ranks the highest, and you will be glad you did.

Chapter 2: Who Do I Need to Pay Besides Employees?

Who will I pay to provide my business with goods and services?

Make an initial assessment of who you will be paying for goods or services to operate your business.

This can vary widely depending on the type of business you are in, but the following are some common examples:

- Accountant or Bookkeeper
- Lawyer

- Insurance Agent
- Banker
- Website designer
- Graphic Designer or Printer
- Technical support person

You may not need all of these, and there may be others you need to include. Make a list of everyone you will need to pay.

Identify who will fill each role and contact them to verify they can provide what you need when you need it.

It's worth your time to ask questions about their processes and procedures.

For example, will there be forms you need to complete before engaging their services? Will that be a one-time thing? That is a contract. Or will it be required each time you utilize their services? That is a work order.

Which of the following three ways will they charge you?

1. <u>Bid or estimate</u>. This approach is based on the work requested. This is often the case with web designers. They would likely meet with you to do a needs analysis and then create a bid or estimate, detailing the cost, hours, and estimated

timeline to complete requested changes to your website. Of course, for minor changes, the process may be simplified.

2. <u>Hourly rates</u>. A graphic designer, for example, may strictly charge by the hour.

3. <u>Recurring fee</u>. This could be a monthly service fee that provides certain services or a certain number of hours. For example, a bookkeeper or accountant may require a monthly fee to balance your books and provide you with standard accounting reports. That is an income statement,

balance sheet, and profit and loss statement. Annual or quarterly tax preparation may be included within that fee or billed as a separate amount.

Before you go into business with any paid provider, be thorough in asking them questions. Below are some examples.

- When was your last rate increase, and how much of an increase was it?

- Are there limits on how often or by how much you increase your rates? If not, would you consider including limits with our arrangement?

- What are your payment terms – net 30 days or something else?

- Do you allow installment payments?

- What is the typical turnaround time on your services?

This isn't a complete list. Use the list to jump-start your thinking on what you want to ask. Be prepared, be thorough, and be consistent in asking your questions.

The people you identify in the next chapter can often provide valuable insights into what to ask your paid providers before you hire them. So, before you interview or hire any paid providers, answer the questions in the next chapter.

Chapter 3: Who Else Can Provide Wisdom and Insights?

Who are my informal advisors?

These are people you trust that are willing to share their business knowledge with you. They are willing and able to provide helpful insights and opinions. They can be people that you pay, but typically they are unpaid.

While all of them don't have to be business owners, make sure at least one of them is. Because they must be willing and able to share their business knowledge, it is unlikely that they would be in direct competition with your business. Much more likely, they would be in a business that compliments yours. If so, and you can collaborate, even better. For example, a realtor and a landscaping business could be great informal advisors for each other.

These must be people you trust, with a good sense regarding business.

They are people that you can run ideas by or help fill in your knowledge gaps. For example, if you don't have much marketing experience, you will want someone to advise you in that area.

Generally speaking, you'll meet with your informal advisors individually, but if you'd rather meet with multiple advisors at a time, that can be effective too.

Before you hire your paid partners, ask your informal advisors what questions to ask. Your informal advisors will have insights and knowledge. If they don't, choose different advisors. Don't be shy about asking for their opinions and insights. Tap into their knowledge and share your knowledge with them. Pay it forward whenever you can by sharing your knowledge beyond just your informal advisors.

Chapter 4: Make it Legal

Which legal form of business structure will I use?

There are several different ways you can structure your business. Here are some:

- Sole proprietor

- Limited Liability Company, commonly called an LLC

- Partnership

- S-Corp

- Corporation

Depending on your needs, there are advantages and disadvantages to each. Ask your informal advisors for insights here if you wish. But you must discuss this with at least two of your paid providers. That is, your tax person and lawyer. They will help you determine the best legal form to use, given your specific situation.

Chapter 5: Is it Needed?

Is there a <u>real need</u> for what I am offering?

This question, along with the next two, seem like no-brainers. It is easy to gloss over them and not put much thought into your answers. Don't do it.

Why do I say that? Well, let's think about it. If you ignore this question and there isn't a real need for what you're offering, what will happen? You'll spend lots of time and money on your business and likely have to shut down. You will be emotionally and financially stressed about something you could have avoided. Instead, save yourself time and money and reduce your stress by answering this question completely and honestly.

We all tend to fall in love with our ideas. This can blind us to reality, making it difficult to answer this question honestly.

It's easy to get swept up by an idea that is unique or clever. Remember, no matter how unique or clever your idea is, there still needs to be a real business need to create profit.

A key quality of a successful business owner is the ability to be brutally honest with yourself. Be brutally honest when answering all of these questions and enjoy the success it brings.

There are three possible answers to the question in this chapter:

1. No, there isn't a need.

2. Yes, there is a need, but it isn't obvious to prospects.

3. Yes, there is a need, and the people with the need are aware of it.

Do your research to determine if there is a real need. This could involve such things as conducting surveys, doing market research, or forming focus groups.

After you've done your research, you may find there isn't a need. That is, you don't have a viable business idea. Don't lose faith. Your research may have uncovered the "gold" that shows you how to tweak your idea so that it becomes a viable business idea.

If the answer comes back as #2, you can still have a viable business. However, you'll need to modify your plan to include time and resources to educate people about their need for your offering. As a result, your business will likely take longer to gain traction. It can also increase your initial or ongoing expenses. Instead of being discouraged by this, just factor it into your planning.

The ideal answer, of course, is #3, that people are aware of the need. If your research lands you here, then great. Just remember that when the potential customers know that there's a need, that likely means you already have several competitors (or soon will). This means you will need to spend sufficient time researching your competition.

Understanding your competitors can be just as important as understanding your customers.

Chapter 6: Ability to Pay

<u>Can</u> they pay for what I am offering?

Let's say, for example, you want to start a business as a career coach.

I anticipate you have seen the statistics that most people are unhappy in their work. A Forbes article claims that over half of U.S. workers are unhappy (Kelly, 2019). The need exists for career coaches.

But if you are focusing on people who have been downsized, they may have a strong need but be unable to pay for your products or services.

Determine that a real need exists AND that your prospects can pay.

Chapter 7: Will They Pay?

<u>Will</u> they pay for what I am offering?

This question is harder to answer. Just because they have the need and the money doesn't mean they will part with the money.

They must see that the money they pay you will return at least that much value to them. If they don't see that or see someone else provide more value for the same money, it's unlikely you'll get their business.

Also, they must rank this need higher than their other needs. For example, if they are ranking spending money for your services vs. taking a family vacation, the vacation will likely win out.

Of course, it's all a matter of context. Suppose your service is air conditioning repair. A family in Arizona with a broken air conditioner will likely give that priority over a family vacation (sorry, kids).

Another consideration is how will your product or service make them feel. Again, I will use coaching as an example. With coaching, you are usually helping someone make a change. This means leaving their comfort zone.

They will be spending money on a service that will create uncomfortable feelings. This is another level of complexity that can reduce their willingness to spend money. However, this can be overcome by changing the prospect's focus. That is, get them to focus more on how they'll feel <u>after</u> making the change instead of how they will feel <u>during</u> the change.

If, however, your business is wedding photography, it's almost a given that the prospect will pay. It's just a question of whether they will pay you or a competitor.

Think of questions five, six, and seven as being connected. That is, is there a <u>real need</u>, AND <u>can</u> they pay, AND <u>will</u> they pay? All three answers must be "yes" to have a viable business.

Chapter 8: Competition

How much competition will I have?

Most people assume less competition is good and that no competition is great. But no competition may be a bigger problem than too much.

Yes, too much competition can be challenging. How do I break through the crowd to be visible and recognized as offering unique value? But if there is no competition, how can that be a problem?

Well, if there is no competition, it may mean there isn't a need for what you want to offer.

Regardless of how much or how little competition you have, it is critical that you do your research before launching.

You can send out surveys, do test marketing, or form focus groups. These things don't need to cost a lot of money or involve a lot of time.

The key takeaway is don't ever skip the research step due to limited competition. Instead, tailor your research to match the amount of competition. For example, if there is a lot of competition, you'll want to focus more on understanding your competitors. That is, you need to know what they're doing well and <u>not</u> doing well. This helps you see ways to differentiate yourself from the competition.

If, however, there is little or no competition, your focus will be more on understanding the marketplace, the prospects' needs, and why there isn't more competition. You would also focus on understanding where your perceived offering ranks within your customer's budget and what features or options could cause it to rank higher. Regardless, you'll need to research all the areas listed above. Use the amount of competition as an indicator to help you determine which areas to focus on the most.

If there is little or no competition in your chosen field, this research will help you understand why. Does it mean there isn't a need? Or that the competition exists, but it simply isn't obvious? Or is the cost to enter this marketplace too high? If so, how do you plan to overcome that?

These are just a few possible reasons. The bottom line is, you need to figure out the reason or reasons so you know whether to move forward with your business idea or not.

For the analysis I'm suggesting here, the focus is on your direct competition. That is, businesses offering products or services similar to yours.

There will be times to focus on your indirect competition too. Indirect competition is a business that is unlike yours, but a prospect may choose to spend money with them instead of with you.

For example, a company that refinishes kitchen cabinets could tie up money from your prospect that prevents them from hiring you to, say, tutor their teenage son in math.

Before doing a full-blown launch of your business, do your research and do it in ways that don't cost you a lot of time or money.

Chapter 9: Plan B and Beyond

What is my financial fallback if things go slower than planned?

I hope your business launch is a huge success from the start and stays that way.

Realistically, that won't happen for everyone. It's good to have a Plan B in case your original plan doesn't turn out as expected.

In other words, do you have money in savings you can use if things go more slowly than planned?

Will you continue to work either a part-time or full-time job during the initial launch of your business?

It's a big risk to quit your job without any savings or another source of income. That source could be a working spouse or life partner, for example. Having at least one continuing income stream is good. More than one is even better.

Chapter 10: Self-Employment

Have I ever been self-employed before?

If so, what are the key lessons you learned, and how can you apply them now?

If not, what have you done to learn more about self-employment? Seminars, books, and classes are a great place to start when you don't have experience.

Also, which of your informal advisors is self-employed? Tap into their experience to learn what you can. Be sure at least one of your informal advisors is or has been self-employed. More than one is ideal.

Remember, your learning won't stop once you launch. To succeed as a small business owner, commit to being a life-long learner.

Chapter 11: Business Model

What business model will I use?

There are many to choose from. Here are a few:

- Physical location, that is, a storefront

- Online-based

- Network Marketing or Multi-Level Marketing, this may also be called an MLM

- Franchise

- Low-cost

- High-quality

- Free intro/paid upgrade

- Subscription or membership

I anticipate that you are familiar with nearly all of these models. The one model that may not sound familiar initially is the free intro/paid upgrade. A great example of this is with apps for your smartphone. Often an introductory version of the app, with reduced functionality, is available for free. To get the full-featured version, you have to pay to upgrade.

Keep in mind, the list above isn't a comprehensive one. Also, you may end up using a combination of these models. The good news is you don't have to figure out all the variations immediately. But you do need to pick one model to launch with. Start simple by choosing one model. If you want, you can add variations later, once your business is more established.

Below is an example of what this could look like. Before launch, you decide your primary method is an online business. Then six months or a year later, you may decide to add a membership-based service. The appeal of a membership model is often the exclusive nature of it. It is often promoted as a VIP type of membership. This can be offered as tiered levels of membership. While you may use other terminology, the basic concept is often called bronze, silver, and gold-level memberships.

Chapter 12: Ideal Customer

Who is my ideal customer?

Tip: Create a spreadsheet for questions 12, 13, and 14. List the questions you've come up with down the left-hand side. Then your column headings would be the type of customer: ideal, good, and nightmare.

Write down who your ideal customer is. Below are sample questions to get you started. Some of these questions may be hard to answer, but just do the best you can. Keep in mind that while you want to be as specific with your answers as possible, some of these answers will be rough approximations.

For example, let's use the number of children. Let's say you identify your ideal customer as "having one to two children." But you may also see that your product or service could be a fit for someone with no children or more than two children. They would be considered a good customer. This will be covered in more detail in the next chapter.

Of course, if your product or service is directly related to children, then your answer will likely be different. Maybe it would be more along the lines of: "My ideal customer will have one or more children or one or more grandchildren."

Consider the following questions as a starting point in identifying your ideal customer:

- What is their gender?
- What age range do they fall into? You will define the ranges.
- What level of education do they have?
- Do they have children?
    - How many children?
    - What ages are they?

- What range does their income fall into? You will define the ranges.

- Are they employed?

    o Roughly how many hours a week do they work?

    o What is their normal work shift?

    o Do they have one or multiple jobs?

    o Do they work for someone else, are they self-employed, or is it both?

- Where do they spend most of their free time?

- What are their hobbies?

- Roughly how much disposable income do they have?

The more you know about your ideal customer, the easier it is to speak their language and attract them to your products and services. Use whichever of these questions you find useful and add questions of your own.

Chapter 13: Good Customer

Who isn't an ideal customer but would still be a good customer to have?

Now that you've identified your ideal customer dial it back a bit and define who would be a good customer.

They aren't quite the ideal customer, but you still want to do business with them.

Use similar questions as you used for the ideal customer; answer them for a good customer instead.

Your marketing and promotional efforts will primarily target your ideal customer but may also attract those in the good customer group.

Another way to define a good customer is that you aren't necessarily seeking them out, but you will want to do business with them if they find you.

Chapter 14: Nightmare Customer

What qualities would a nightmare customer have?

Now define what your nightmare customer looks like. This is the person that makes you want to tear your hair out.

It may seem odd that I am asking you to define your nightmare customer, but there is a valid reason. Know what's important to your nightmare customer to limit how many you attract.

When you create a marketing or promotional piece, review it against the spreadsheet I mentioned in question 12. It needs to "check all the boxes" for your ideal customer and few or none of the boxes for your nightmare customer. If that's not the case, then make adjustments, so it is. Use a similar review process for any new product, new service, and changes to your website.

Keep in mind this works both ways. For example, if your new product or service doesn't match your ideal customer, you have three possible choices. One is to adjust the product or service to match the spreadsheet. Or, two, adjust the spreadsheet to match your product or service. In this case, the qualities of your ideal customer have changed somewhat. Or, three, adjust both the spreadsheet and the product or service.

The point is, don't automatically change one or the other. Spend the time to think it through.

Chapter 15: Get the Best, Forget the Rest

What plans will I put in place to limit the nightmare customers while increasing the ideal and good customers?

This is your ultimate goal, isn't it? Maximize the number of ideal and good customers while minimizing the number of nightmare customers.

Ok, I'll admit the title of this chapter isn't 100% accurate. All of your customers may not be "the best." But the point is to be selective.

Analyze your ideal, good, and nightmare customer profiles to determine where you should focus your efforts and where you shouldn't.

New business owners often make a big mistake by offering a product or service for free or heavily discounted. I did it when I first started. A much better alternative is to offer add-ons. More on that later in this chapter.

When you offer a huge discount or something for free – it often means you attract a less desirable customer. This may mean an increase in complaints.

Whenever I offered significant discounts, I always saw an increase in complaints. I've heard many similar stories from other business owners. I realize it sounds counter-intuitive, but it is true. Like it or not, offering a significant discount can work against you.

This doesn't mean that you never offer discounts or make free offers. Instead, it just means that you think it through very carefully. For example, offering a free eBook on your website in exchange for those who sign up for your newsletter is a solid business idea. It is a low risk for complaints because if someone doesn't like the newsletter, they simply unsubscribe.

Also, add-ons tend to be a better business strategy than discounting. For example, if you offer skin care products, you could include a free lip balm with every order over a certain threshold, say $30. Or, if you're a consultant, you could offer seven months of consulting for the price of six months, for example. Or you could include a complimentary follow-up session, say three months after your consulting is complete. There are many options when it comes to add-ons.

A place where you often see add-ons is with an air conditioning repair and replacement. The add-on may take the form of a warranty or a follow-up service call. Add-ons are almost always a better choice than discounts.

Chapter 16: Define Your Absolutes

What are my customer absolutes?

It isn't enough to know your ideal customer. You need to know your customer absolutes too.

What do I mean by customer absolutes? These are the qualities a customer must have, or you won't work with them.

This will vary significantly depending on the type of business you have. For example, if you are going to run a landscaping service, your only absolutes may be that they own the property and will pay.

As a coach, one of my absolutes is that the person must be open to change. I tell them that right up front. If they aren't open to change, I won't take them on as a client.

Tip: Add a column for customer absolutes to the spreadsheet you created for questions 12, 13, and 14.

Chapter 17: What's Unique?

What makes my business and offerings unique?

This is often one of the most difficult things for a business owner to define. Regardless, it's very important.

If you've got a unique product, service, or business approach, that's great. That isn't always the case. But even if it is the case for you, the odds are that the uniqueness won't last long. Your success will be noticed and imitated in some form by other businesses. So, no matter how unique your situation is, it's worthwhile to answer this question as completely as you can.

How is my product, service, or approach different from my competitors?

The more precisely you can define this, the more effective your website and other marketing materials will be in clearly conveying why a prospect should work with you instead of your competitors.

It is easy to think that the key differentiator is you. In other words, my business has me, and that's a difference-maker. Sorry, but that isn't a sufficient answer to this question. Let's face it, unless your prospect knows you personally, just having you won't be enough to sway them. Go deeper and ask yourself what qualities, education, and experience you have that makes working with you a better choice.

It can be frustrating trying to define this but stick with it. Be thorough because it can be the difference between success and failure.

Not to sound dramatic, but if you can't clearly define this, how will you stand out from your competitors? If your prospects can't clearly see the difference, it will turn into a price war. Few businesses survive a price war.

Chapter 18: Customer Interactions

Where will I interact with my customers?

This often ties in directly to what business model you have chosen.

Some examples of where you might interact with your customers include your store/office/home, their office/home, online (website, zoom, or chat), or a neutral location, such as a coffee shop or rented or leased meeting space.

You need to identify all the locations and assign a rough percentage to each.

For example, if you have a physical location, a storefront, do you anticipate 95% of your business be done in person and 5% via the web? Or will the mix be more like 70/30 or something else?

Initially, this will just be your best guess. But you'll want to track the actual numbers ongoing. Then your future planning will be made using the actual numbers.

Take the time to think through where you'll interact with your customers and the relative mix of each. This is important because it drives other aspects of your business. For instance, issues related to inventory, marketing, communication methods, and hiring, to name a few.

At this stage, these are just educated guesses. But it is important that you at least have an estimate. A few examples of why it is important:

- How much inventory should you stock initially?

    o How will you determine your reorder points? What system will you use to track inventory?

- What will you charge for shipping fees?

- Will you ship internationally or just domestically?

- Who will pack and ship the orders?

    o You?

    o Employees?

    o A third party?

- Will you need to hire employees?

    o Will they be part-time, full-time, seasonal, or a mix?

    o If they're full-time, will you administer their benefit programs or outsource it to a third party?

- How will you utilize your web site?

    o Will you sell products online? If so, your site will need to handle order processing. If order processing isn't needed, the focus would be much different, more focused on driving customers to your physical location, announcing new products, and announcing upcoming events, for example.

Chapter 19: Social Media Platform Strategy: Narrow vs. Wide

What is my primary social media platform?

You will likely be using multiple social media platforms. However, it's best to pick one as your primary. Base it on the type of business and customers you have.

For example, if your customers are other businesses, that is Business to Business or B2B, LinkedIn may be a good primary social media channel.

But if you are mostly selling to consumers, that is, Business to Consumer or B2C, your primary platform may be one of the following: Facebook, Instagram, Pinterest, or Twitter.

Choosing a primary social media platform is a function of knowing who your customers are and which platform they would most likely gravitate toward. The better job you do of defining your customers, the easier it will be to choose a primary social media platform.

There is a common belief that you must be on every possible social media platform. It's a bad idea because it is like thinking everyone is a potential customer. It dilutes your message and your focus. Successful businesses don't try to be all things to all people. Instead, they focus on a certain niche. It doesn't mean that you can't have customers outside of that niche. You can and can serve more than one niche. But initially, make your focus narrow. This will make it significantly easier to grow and establish your business.

Initially, limit yourself to three social media platforms at the most. Choose one as your primary based on where your potential customers will most likely be found.

Chapter 20: Product, Service, or Both?

Will I be offering products, services, or both?

Make a list of all the products and services you will be offering initially. Over time, you will add to the list and subtract from it.

Keep the initial list as concise as possible. Resist the urge to think more is better. Get your initial offerings established first. Once that is done, then and only then should you think about adding more offerings.

At the start of your business, keep your focus on making your initial products and services the best they can be for your customers. With a small list, it will be much easier to make any needed adjustments. Also, you'll be more agile in responding to the needs of your customers and the market. This can be a competitive advantage.

Don't look at expanding your list of offerings until your initial offerings are stable.

It's a good idea to put this information into a spreadsheet. Then it is easy to include things like:

- Pricing

- The date you started offering it
- The date you quit offering it
- Target audience
- What kind of margin you built into the product or the service
- Any introductory specials you offered. For example, the details of the offer, duration, customer response, etc.
- Other notes

Chapter 21: Offering Guarantees?

Will I offer any guarantees?

Determine this before you launch because you want to communicate it to prospects.

If you're offering a guarantee, use it to promote your product or service in your marketing materials and on your website.

If you aren't offering a guarantee, you want people to know that too.

For example, before I work with a new coaching client, we review a coaching agreement document. We discuss the key points of the agreement that is in front of us, both signing it. One of those key points is a statement that says coaching results aren't guaranteed.

This may sound foolish. However, guaranteeing something you can't deliver is even more foolish. I don't have control over how willing that person is to change. Of course, I will do what I can to influence that person's desire to change. But, ultimately, they are the one who decides whether they'll put in the effort or not.

If I were to guarantee coaching results, that would put me outside of integrity. So, I won't do it. I do guarantee that I will put every effort into helping them make progress toward their goals. That statement is included in the coaching agreement. That is something I have control over, so guaranteeing it makes sense.

Chapter 22: Returns and Warranties

What are my policies for returns and warranties?

Returns can become very complicated very quickly. Knowing your policy upfront, and making sure your customers do, is key to limiting headaches and misunderstandings later on.

If you offer returns on any of your products, some of the questions you will need to answer are:

- Is there a restocking fee, or will the customer get a 100% refund?

- Is there a deadline for returns? For example, do they only have 30, 60, or 90 days to return the product, or is it longer?

- If there is a deadline, is it based on the order date or the date the product was shipped?

- What are the conditions of the return? Does the package have to be unopened or the product unused? Or will you have no such conditions? If it is open or used, will the refund be full, partial, or no refund at all?

- Who pays shipping fees on a returned item, you or the customer?

- Will you do tiered returns? For example, a 100% refund within the first 30 days, a 75% refund after 30 days, etc.

Include your return and warranty policies on your website and on your invoices.

Also, include an FAQ section on your website. FAQ stands for Frequently Asked Questions. Here you will answer the most common questions that customers may have. Besides other topics, you would also want to answer common questions about returns and warranties here.

You will need someone to review your policies and any digital or printed text related to warranties. If your lawyer has experience in this area, have them do it.

If your lawyer doesn't have experience with warranties, ask them and your informal advisors who they'd recommend.

Chapter 23: Billing and Payments

How will I process billing and payments?

How will you bill clients by the hour or by the project?

Will you give a discount if they pay in cash? If so, how much?

Will you allow installment payments? That is, do they have to pay it all at once, or can they split it into multiple payments? For example, can they split it into monthly payments? If so, how many months will you allow them to spread it over?

What types of payment will you accept? Cash, check, or credit card? Will you accept online payments? Paypal is one of the most well-known options for secure online payments. The list of options for online payments changes frequently, so I won't attempt to include a complete list of options here. Instead, a few of the other options you might consider include Square, Stripe, Amazon Pay, Google Pay, and Apple Pay.

But the bottom line is, the better you know your customers and potential customers, the better you can choose payment options that appeal to them. I'd suggest starting small, with just a few payment options initially. You can add other options later if needed.

What will your process be for late payments? Will you charge them interest? If so, how much? At what point will you turn a late payment over to a collection agency? Whatever you decide, you'll want to include the late payment terms on your invoice and your website. Use your lawyer to help with the wording.

You'll need to document these policies for yourself and any employees.

Chapter 24: Define Security Measures

What security measures do I need to consider?

There are six broad areas of security you should consider:

1. Inventory controls. If you are selling a product, you will need security measures to track your inventory to ensure none of it goes missing.

2. Building access. If you plan to have a physical store, you will need security to prevent people from wandering into areas they shouldn't and

prevent unauthorized access when you are closed.

If you own the building, it will be up to you to determine which of the following you need, security access cards, security cameras, and alarm systems. A wide variety of door and window locks are available. You may want to consult with your insurance agent and possibly a locksmith as well.

If you will be leasing, ask your prospective landlord to see a detailed report of what security measures are included with the building before signing the lease.

It's best to avoid leasing a building where you need to install additional security measures. If you pursue such a lease, be sure all the details are in writing. Specifically, you want the answers to the following questions specified in the lease.

- What can be installed?
- Who pays for the equipment?
- Who pays for the installation?

- Who owns it after the lease ends?

Also, have your lawyer review all leasing documents and give you their assessment before you sign.

3. <u>Financial records</u>. These records can be stored on paper, in a computer system, or both. The next section talks specifically about computer security. As such, there may be some overlap between this section and the next one.

You need security for financial records on two levels. On one level, you need security measures that prevent employees from manipulating data to steal from you.

On a second level, you need security measures that ensure data is only seen by people who have a valid reason to see it. Be sure all digital records are password protected. Keep paper records in a locked file, with a limited number of people having access to the key.

4. <u>Computer security</u>. You need to be concerned about both internal and external security. Internal security is

what prevents employees from accessing parts of your systems they don't have clearance for. External security is making sure outsiders can't hack into your systems. Unless you are very well-versed in technology, you will want to have a technical person as one of your paid providers. Prepare a list of questions before your initial meeting with them. Be sure to ask them how often they recommend conducting a security review or audit to ensure your security measures remain effective. If they say ongoing security reviews aren't needed, I'd strongly suggest finding a different technical expert. Over time, there will be changes in technology, hackers' methods, business needs, and standard security measures. These are all reasons to have regularly scheduled security reviews.

There is no hard-and-fast rule about how often to conduct security reviews. A rough guideline is to conduct one every 12 – 18 months. If you've recently installed a lot of new software or have circumstances prone to being hacked, conducting a security review more often may make sense.

An example of circumstances prone to being hacked is doing a lot of credit card business.

Besides knowing the technology, your technical person should also make solid recommendations on security policies. Some examples are

- Determining the frequency for security reviews.

- Recommending the number of unique

security profiles to set up for your employees.

- Determining which files and systems will require password protection.

- Recommending which antivirus and internet firewall software best meet your needs.

- Helping you determine appropriate data encryption and archival procedures.

Whether you have employees or not, data encryption will need to be addressed. That is, what level of encryption is appropriate for the various types of data on your systems. It is easy to think you can ignore encryption, but don't do it. News stories are common about data breaches in large organizations creating a big negative impact. Large organizations usually have enough resources to bounce back from that, but at a high cost, including a tarnished reputation and lost revenue. However, for a smaller business, a single data breach can put you out of business.

5. Client information. Your clients will be trusting you to keep their information safe. Keep client paperwork under lock and key and encrypt all digital data. Also, make sure all computers and network access require a password. Invest in a good paper shredder too.

6. Credit card information. Whether you are processing credit cards in person or online, you need security in place in both situations. Credit card information is highly prized by hackers. Have procedures in place to ensure any paperwork with

credit card information is shredded as soon as it can be.

Tip: Provide your insurance agent with a list of the security measures you will be implementing. It may lower your insurance costs. Ask your agent to review the list and suggest what other measures you can put in place to lower your risk.

Chapter 25: Insurance Needs

What types of insurance will I need?

Check with your insurance agent to determine the types of insurance you may need. Some things to consider are:

- If you are providing a product, you might need product liability insurance.

- If you have a service business, you may need personal liability insurance.

- If you use a vehicle to transport your product or

deliver a service, your insurance will need to reflect that.

- If you own a building that you will use for your business, you will likely need property insurance.

- If you are leasing a building, you may need insurance for contents and inventory. Check with your landlord to determine what insurance coverage, if any, is provided with your lease. You don't want to be under-insured or to have double coverage.

- If your legal form of business is a partnership, you will

need to have a life insurance policy insuring the partners.

- If you have employees, you may need to provide medical insurance, workman's compensation insurance, etc.

These are just some examples of issues to consider. The point is, take the time to prepare a list of questions. Then meet with your insurance agent to review those questions and the specifics of your business. Your agent will help you determine what types of coverage you'll need.

Chapter 26: Determine the End Game

What is my exit strategy?

At some point, you will be parting ways with your business. Maybe you'll want to open a new business, go work for someone else, or retire. Your business could be sold, passed along to a family member, or just closed down.

No matter what, it's good to know your exit strategy before you even start. I can assure you that it will be much easier to think through and decide this now instead of later.

First, there can be tax implications. The sooner you know the tax implications and make a plan, the better.

Second, your desired exit strategy may influence which business model you choose.

Third, your business will keep you busy. So, the more decisions you can make before launch, the better.

Fourth, if you wait until later to decide, it will likely be a more stressful time. Also, there may be pressure to decide quickly. Suppose you receive a job offer that you have to respond to within 72 hours. Or what if an opportunity comes along to start a new business that you need to act quickly upon. Making those decisions and adapting to those changes will be enough of a challenge. You don't need the added challenge of determining how to transition out of your current business. Do yourself a favor and figure out that part now.

Some questions to consider include: Will you sell the business? Shut it down? Will a family member inherit it?

If it's a partnership:

- Will the other partner have an option to buy you out and take over as the sole owner?

- Will there be an option for someone else to step into your shoes as the new partner?

- Will the business be dissolved or sold?

Before you launch your business, discuss your exit strategy options with your accounting person and your lawyer. Knowing the tax and legal implications upfront will help you make better decisions and create a smooth transition later on.

Chapter 27: Initial Metrics

What indicators will I use to tell me if my business will make it or not?

It's tempting to skip this question. After all, you're excited about your business, and this question dampens that enthusiasm, right? But you need to consider these issues now because waiting makes it increasingly more difficult to address.

This question is one of the toughest ones. It almost sounds like planning to fail. But it's not. This is truly about being realistic and prepared. Ideally, your business will thrive. But it might not.

For this question, analyze and decide what criteria you will use to measure your business's success. The criteria can be a combination of things. It is often a combination of time and money.

For example, your criteria could be: After 18 months, my business will have started to make a profit. This is just one example. What you choose might be something completely different. The key is to choose something you are comfortable with and stick to it.

Once your business has launched, it's easy to tell yourself success is right around the corner. I just need that one big client, or my new product or service will fix everything. Or next month will be better.

Those things could be true. But when you're busy running your business, it's much harder to see these things clearly. It's much easier to tell yourself to keep going even if the numbers say otherwise.

Determine your metrics before you launch because you'll be more objective. Why will you be more objective before launch? Because you haven't put near as much time into your business now as you will have later. That's why it's so important to know these answers now.

Also, once you're up and running, you'll be even more passionate about your business. Passion is good, but it also has a downside. Passion can blind you to rational thought. It is easy to fool yourself that you are looking at things rationally, even when you aren't.

Do yourself a favor and decide before you launch what metrics you'll use. Use these metrics to determine the threshold between continuing in business and pulling the plug.

Thinking of these things now can be a bit of a downer. But try to think of it instead as just a part of your preparation and planning. The more you have thought through what failure looks like, the better prepared you will be to avoid it.

Summary

There you have it, 27 questions to ask yourself before you launch your business. It's a lot to take in, right?

It may seem overwhelming and a bit discouraging. But remember, my goal with this book was to be thorough and arm you with all the information you might need. As such, you may have read some things you never even considered before.

Take the time to absorb what you've read here. Some of what I covered may not apply to you. For example, if you don't have employees initially, that simplifies things.

This book is a bit like drinking from a firehose. There's so much. It's hard to take it all in at once. Take your time and review it as you proceed forward. Determine what applies to your situation and what doesn't. Be thoughtful and take a systematic approach.

Invest the time to answer each of these questions as honestly and completely as you can.

As you prepare to launch, add other questions and answers you believe will help.

Don't skip the tough questions. That's where you'll learn the most. In our culture, where everyone is looking to do things faster, don't look for a shortcut here. Be thorough.

I strongly encourage you to record your answers. There isn't a valid reason not to have your answers documented digitally, given the great technologies available to us. For example, the voice typing feature of google documents will type your words as you speak them.

I'd like to put in a quick plug to encourage you to write a business plan. Writing a business plan has come to be seen as a waste of time by many. As a result, many businesses launch without ever having created any sort of business plan.

If you're looking for financing for your business, your lender will likely require a business plan.

But even if you aren't looking for financing, I'd encourage you to complete a business plan. It can be an informal plan and doesn't need to take much time.

Go against the grain and create a business plan. It is one simple way to get an edge on your competition. There are many great online tools to simplify this process.

Find a free or low-cost tool you like and take the time to write your business plan. I think you'll discover that you'll gain clarity about what you want to accomplish and how you'll want to go about it.

And lastly, don't stop asking yourself questions. That could be adding to this list of 27 questions before you launch or continuing to ask yourself questions ongoing. Either way, it's important to keep asking those questions.

By continuing to ask yourself questions, you will continue to improve and adapt your business.

Doing so will create even greater success for yourself and your customers.

Appendix: Recommended Reading

The following are all great books but with a list this long, where to start?

Starting with whatever grabs your attention is always a good approach. But if you're still unsure, I'd suggest the following three books are a good starting point.

Refuse to Choose: Use All of Your Interests, Passions, and Hobbies to Create the Life and Career of Your Dreams by Barbara Sher

Making a Living Without a Job by Barbara Winter

This Time I Dance: Creating the Work You Love by Tama Kieves

The remaining books are also packed with helpful information.

Deep Work: Rules for Focused Success in a Distracted World by Cal Newport

Leadership and Self-Deception by The Arbinger Institute

The Little Book of Talent by Daniel Coyle

The Magic of Thinking Big by David J. Schwartz

Manage Your Day-To-Day: Build Your Routine, Find Your Focus &

Sharpen Your Creative Mind by 99U

The Myth of Multitasking by Dave Crenshaw

Presence: Bringing Your Boldest Self to Your Biggest Challenges by Amy Cuddy

Show Your Work by Austin Kleon

Steal Like an Artist by Austin Kleon

About the Author

Bob is the author of multiple books and has a background in education, management, coaching, and technology. He loves to travel, meet new people, read, and listen to music. Any day he can make someone laugh or smile is a darn good day. He lives in sunny Tucson, Arizona.

Other Books by Bob

Making the Shift to Online Learning: 5 Keys to Success

Mindset Makeover: How Small Changes Can Unlock Your Potential

Divorce: Learning to Heal and Grow

Toss Those Resolutions: Why It's Time to Give Them Up and What to Do Instead

Woody Two Shoes: New Shoes for Woody

Acknowledgments

First, I want to thank those business owners and future business owners that I taught and coached. Putting your faith and trust in me means more than you'll ever know. Your zeal for your ideas and desire to build something uniquely yours has helped keep my lamp lit.

Thanks to Pradeep from CoverCreators for designing such a beautiful cover.

Also, I'd like to thank Heather Bennett and Ryan Christensen for their edits and feedback.

I'm sending my heartfelt thanks to you, my readers, as well. Thanks for being supportive, so I can continue engaging with the true joy that writing adds to my life.

References

Blank, S. (2010). No plan survives first contact with customers – Business plans versus business models. Retrieved from https://steveblank.com/2010/04/08/no-plan-survives-first-contact-with-customers-%E2%80%93-business-plans-versus-business-models/

Kelly, J. (2019). More than half of U.S. workers are unhappy in their jobs: Here's why and what needs to be done now. Retrieved from https://www.forbes.com/sites/jackkelly/2019/10/25/more-than-half-of-us-workers-are-unhappy-in-their-jobs-heres-why-and-what-needs-to-be-done-now/#4d511b282024

www.ingramcontent.com/pod-product-compliance
Lightning Source LLC
Chambersburg PA
CBHW060846220526
45466CB00003B/1255